# The Queen & Her Family

## A PICTORIAL RECORD

# 'The Family Firm'

King George VI, it is said, liked to refer to the British monarchy as 'the Family Firm'; more recently an American television commentator spoke of 'those hard-working Windsors'. Both references are apt.

The monarchy is indeed a family concern, long established in British history. From the accession of William the Conqueror in 1066 it has passed by bloodline (albeit at times tenuously, but never broken) through seven dynasties and 40 incumbents to the present monarch, Queen Elizabeth II.

In regard to the American television comment: in 1986 'those hard-working Windsors' carried out more than 2,500 public engagements, The Queen herself undertaking some 430 of these as well as, with Prince Philip, spending nearly six weeks abroad on official tours to Nepal, New Zealand, Australia, China and Hong Kong.

The present world-wide fascination with the Royal Family stems from the personalities of its members and the ease of travel and communication in the 1980s. Today The Queen is never more than a day's flight away from the

most remote corner of the Commonwealth and during her reign she has visited every Commonwealth country and many foreign lands.

Millions of visitors are attracted to Britain to see the pomp and splendour that surrounds the monarchy and modern television technology takes this colourful ceremonial right into the homes of countless more people round the world. This is specially true of such major events as the Royal Weddings of the Prince and Princess of Wales in St. Paul's Cathedral (when there was an estimated television audience of 750 million) and of the Duke and Duchess of York in Westminster Abbey.

The Queen herself has done much to make royalty less remote and to bring the Royal Family closer to the people.

ABOVE: *The Queen and the Duke of Edinburgh leaving St. George's Chapel Windsor, after one of Britain's most ancient royal ceremonies, the Garter service. On the left the Prince of Wales chats to the Queen Mother while on the right the Knights of the Garter line the chapel steps. Membership of the Order, a gift from the Sovereign, is regarded as the highest distinction.*

Informal 'walkabouts' – a term first used during a tour of New Zealand in 1970 – are now taken for granted on all royal visits. Not without the misgivings of the more security-minded members of her staff, Her Majesty has insisted on meeting the people face to face in as friendly and relaxed an atmosphere as possible.

And yet, despite this increasing informality and exposure, the Royal Family has retained the mystique with which the British and many foreign peoples have always regarded all things royal. Although this could be partly due to the continuing emphasis on pageantry and tradition, it must also have much to do with respect and affection. That recent generations of the Royal Family have preferred to devote their lives to public service rather than to their own pursuits has helped to build the firm foundation on which the stability and popularity of the monarch now stands. Through their own individual talents each member of the Royal Family has contributed something special to the life of the nation and the Commonwealth, and their achievements, by any standards, are remarkable.

# Constitutional Monarch

*'Elizabeth the Second, by the Grace of God, of the United Kingdom of Great Britain and Northern Ireland and of Her other Realms and Territories Queen, Head of the Commonwealth, Defender of the Faith.'*

Such are The Queen's style and titles as used in the United Kingdom, although they differ in each Commonwealth country of which she is Sovereign. Under the British Constitution, the Sovereign remains head of state and retains certain prerogatives, but in practice she entrusts the executive power to her Ministers of the Crown. It is the Sovereign who appoints the Prime Minister, but in the exercise of all other constitutional powers she acts on the advice of the government of the day. These powers include the summoning, prorogation and dissolution of Parliament; the declaration of war and the making of peace; the recognition of foreign states and governments; the concluding of treaties and the annexing or ceding of territories. The Sovereign is head of the judiciary, commander-in-chief of the armed services and temporal governor of the established Church of England. All bills require the Royal Assent before becoming law. The Queen makes formal appointments to all the important offices of state and in the armed services and the Church of England, and she confers peerages, knighthoods and other honours. Her formal approval to all decisions under royal prerogative is given at meetings of the Privy Council ('The Queen in Council').

However, it should not be thought that the Sovereign's role is merely to rubber-stamp decisions of the government. In his famous work, *The English*

TOP: *The Queen welcomes in every New Year at Sandringham, her Norfolk home. But even there affairs of state are not far away. The Queen is shown at her desk in Sandringham working on official papers.*

RIGHT: *The Queen keeps herself well informed of government business through regular meetings with her Prime Minister. Here, Mrs Margaret Thatcher welcomes The Queen to a dinner at 10 Downing Street.*

FAR RIGHT: *One of the most formal occasions in the royal calendar is the annual State Opening of Parliament when The Queen, regally robed and wearing the Imperial State Crown, reads the speech outlining her government's proposals for the coming session from her throne in the House of Lords.*

LEFT: *The Queen inspecting her Guards at the Trooping the Colour ceremony in June 1986, the last time she rode her famous ceremonial horse Burmese on her Birthday Parade.*

ABOVE: *Four years earlier this historic picture was taken showing the head of the Church of Rome, Pope John Paul II, clasping hands in a gesture of friendship with the head of the Church of England, Queen Elizabeth II, at Buckingham Palace.*

*Constitution* (1867), Walter Bagehot wrote: 'The Sovereign has under a constitutional monarchy such as ours the right to be consulted, the right to encourage, the right to warn.' With these rights goes a duty to advise when necessary because an individual monarch will have built up considerable state knowledge and experience during a reign which is generally considerably longer than the five-year period of office to which a British government is elected. The monarch's detached standpoint above party politics makes his or her advice equally valuable to different governments.

Every day The Queen studies Cabinet papers and Foreign Office despatches and receives a report of the day's proceedings in Parliament from the Vice-Chamberlain of the Household, and she sees the Prime Minister regularly

while the House of Commons is sitting. She is also in constant touch with foreign ambassadors and Commonwealth representatives, all of which makes her one of the best-informed people in the country. Furthermore, through her personal contacts with the heads of other states and her frequent visits abroad, The Queen does much to strengthen ties of friendship with foreign and Commonwealth countries.

But The Queen also has an important symbolic role. Through her hereditary position and the age-old ceremonial which surrounds her, she symbolises the unity of the nation and the continuity of the state over the centuries. In carrying out her numerous public duties she helps to cement that unity and to ensure the survival of the traditional moral values which she and her family continue to represent.

## Defender of the Faith

As the established church of the United Kingdom, the Church of England is inextricably bound to the state. Only a member of this Church can succeed to the throne, and it is the Archbishop of Canterbury who crowns a new king or queen regnant in Westminster Abbey. Archbishops, bishops and deans are appointed by the Sovereign on the advice of the Prime Minister, who in turn consults the archbishops of Canterbury and York on those appointments. All clergy are required to take an oath of allegiance to the Crown, and new bishops make an act of homage to the Sovereign. The Church also has to obtain Parliament's consent to change its forms of worship, and senior bishops are members of the House of Lords. The General Synod, the Parliament of the

Church of England, is opened by the Sovereign every five years.

The Queen has an ecclesiastical household comprising the College of Chaplains (36 chaplains whose duties are chiefly honorary) under the Clerk of the Closet and his deputy, and the chaplains and organists of the Chapels Royal at the Tower of London, St. James's Palace and Hampton Court and other places of worship used by Her Majesty. There are also churches known as Royal Peculiars because they are not subject to the jurisdiction of archbishops or bishops, for example Westminster Abbey and St. George's Chapel, Windsor.

The Queen is a firm believer and goes to church every Sunday, often with members of her family. When staying at Windsor she usually goes to the Royal Chapel of All Saints in Windsor

Great Park, at Sandringham she attends the beautiful little church on the royal estate and when on holiday at Balmoral she goes to Crathie Church. On Christmas Day and Easter Sunday the Royal Family attend a service at St. George's Chapel.

ABOVE: *Three days before Easter, The Queen usually attends one of the nation's great cathedrals for the historic Maundy Thursday service and ceremony. Then she distributes Maundy gifts to the same number of men and women as there are years in her life. In 1986 the ceremony was held at Chichester Cathedral where The Queen is seen with the Lord High Almoner (the Bishop of Rochester), the Dean and the Bishop of Chichester and some of the ceremony's younger participants from local schools.*

## The Queen in the United Kingdom

The Queen's public engagements take her to every part of the United Kingdom and involve her in a very wide range of activity. Reviews of the many regiments of which she is colonel-in-chief, opening new buildings, visiting hospitals, schools, welfare organisations and industry, and attending film premières or sporting events, are only some of these activities. Her presence, or that of another member of the Royal Family, at such events ensures that they receive helpful publicity and recognition.

There are a number of special royal occasions which take place regularly each year. Usually in October or November, unless a General Election has been held, there is the State Open-

ing of Parliament, a glittering ceremony at which The Queen rides in a state carriage from Buckingham Palace and, wearing the Imperial State Crown, delivers a speech from the throne in the House of Lords, outlining the government's proposals for the coming session.

In November, again with other members of the Royal Family, The Queen attends the Remembrance Day service in Whitehall for the dead of the two world wars and lays a wreath at the Cenotaph.

In early June Her Majesty, who is passionately fond of horse-racing and an extremely knowledgeable owner and breeder and an expert horsewoman, goes to the Derby at Epsom. Later that month she is at Windsor for Royal Ascot week, Britain's most fashionable race-meeting. Each afternoon, before the racing begins, members of the Royal Family and their guests drive in open landaus down the racecourse in a colourful procession.

June is also the month of the Trooping the Colour ceremony on Horse Guards Parade, in celebration of the Sovereign's official birthday. It was King Edward VII who began the custom of a moveable official birthday in the summer in the hope of ensuring good weather for the ceremony – his own birthday was in November. Each year The Queen's Colour of a battalion of one of the five regiments of Foot Guards is trooped before The Queen in a spectacular parade. From 1969 until 1986 The Queen rode side-saddle on the famous black Canadian mare 'Burmese'.

Also in the summer The Queen holds three garden parties in the grounds at Buckingham Palace, each of which is attended by about 8,000 guests, giving her the opportunity to meet many more people than would otherwise be possible. People from all walks of life come to admire the lovely gardens and enjoy tea and cakes while listening to a band. A garden party is also held at the Palace of Holyroodhouse in Edinburgh during The Queen's residence in June or July.

Throughout the year investitures are held, at which The Queen awards honours to some 2,000 men and women. Most honours are awarded on the Prime Minister's recommendation, but a few are in The Queen's personal gift. Foremost of these is the Order of the Garter, the oldest order for chivalry, founded by King Edward III in 1348 and usually given to very distinguished statesmen, noblemen, military men and Governors-General. The order is limited to 24 Knights

Companion, in addition to The Queen, who is Sovereign of the Order; the Queen Mother, who is a Lady of the Garter; the Duke of Edinburgh and the Prince of Wales, who are Royal Knights, and a number of foreign sovereigns as Extra Knights or Extra Ladies of the Garter. The Knights gather periodically at Windsor Castle for the investiture of new members, a lunch and the Garter service at St. George's Chapel. The Scottish equivalent of the Order of the Garter is the Order of the Thistle.

Other honours given by The Queen personally are the Order of Merit and the Royal Victorian Order, which is awarded to people who have directly served the Royal Family.

The Queen's work is by no means limited to public appearances. Every day much paperwork requires attention. Letters, telegrams, reports and official documents, not only from the government at home but from all the Commonwealth countries, have to be read and signed. Official correspondence is dealt with by The Queen's Private Secretary, Sir William Heseltine, her Deputy Private Secretary, Robert Fellowes, and her Assistant Private Secretary, Kenneth Scott, while her private correspondence and the many hundreds of letters from children are dealt with by her ladies-in-waiting. Most senior of these is the Mistress of the Robes, the Duchess of Grafton. Under her come two Ladies of the Bedchamber – at present the Marchioness of Abergavenny and the Countess of Airlie – an Extra Lady of the Bedchamber, three Women of the Bedchamber and three Extra Women of the Bedchamber.

Like any other 'firm' the monarchy has to be financed. More than three-quarters of The Queen's expenditure as head of state and of her family in assisting her is met by government departments (for instance, the maintenance of the Royal Yacht *Britannia*, The Queen's Flight, the Royal Train and the upkeep of most of the royal palaces). The rest comes from the Civil List, voted by Parliament and administered by the Keeper of the Privy Purse. The Civil List dates from 1760, when King George III surrendered the revenues of the Crown Estates to the Exchequer in return for an annual payment to meet his own requirements and the expenses of the monarchy. Much of this money goes to pay salaries and expenses for the staff of the Royal Household, which numbers approximately 350 people. In 1987 the total amount of the Civil List was £5,289,500, of which £4,326,100 went to The Queen and the rest was

FACING PAGE, ABOVE: *Few royal visits are complete without the highly popular 'walkabout', and this visit to Bromley in Kent was no exception.*

FACING PAGE, BELOW: *When a visit takes The Queen to Scotland the Royal Company of Archers provide her ceremonial bodyguard. Members of the company wear Border green uniforms and Kilmarnock Bonnets with eagles' feathers, and still proudly carry their longbows and arrows.*

TOP: *One of The Queen's favourite visits is to Royal Ascot each year. Before racing begins she drives in an open landau down the racecourse and is here accompanied by the Duke of Edinburgh and the Duke of Gloucester.*

ABOVE: *The nation's great affection for The Queen was much in evidence during the celebrations for her 60th birthday in 1986. She is seen here at Windsor in the Scottish State Coach.*

divided in varying proportions between the other members. Civil List payments, which are for meeting official expenses, are not taxed but any private income of members of the Royal Family other than The Queen is subject to tax in the usual way. The Prince of Wales's income derives from the Duchy of Cornwall: he contributes 25 per cent of the annual net revenue of the Duchy to the Exchequer in lieu of tax.

## The Queen and the Commonwealth

The Commonwealth is a free association of 49 sovereign independent states and their associated states and dependencies all of which acknowledge The Queen as head of the Commonwealth. However, apart from Britain, she is head of state of only 18 of these, including Australia, Canada and New Zealand. In these countries she is represented by a Governor-General who in all essential respects – apart from the appointment of the Governor-General himself and the awarding of honours, which are The Queen's prerogative – holds the same position in relation to the administration of public affairs as The Queen does in Britain.

Twenty-six member countries are republics and have a president as head of state, while Brunei, Lesotho, Malaysia, Swaziland and Tonga have their own monarchs.

The Commonwealth countries have no common policy, although their leaders meet frequently to consult on major issues. Indeed, the only common denominator is their acceptance of The Queen as the symbol of their free association. Her Majesty takes her responsibility towards the Commonwealth very seriously indeed, believing it to be an important force for peace and stability in the world. With the Duke of Edinburgh, she has therefore visited a number of member countries almost every year since her accession. She also receives visits in return from their heads of state, and broadcasts a Christmas message to them all on television and radio. Over the years she has acquired a remarkable working knowledge of the member countries and the problems their leaders face.

The Queen's Commonwealth visits take place at the invitation of the countries concerned, after preliminary consultation with the Foreign and Commonwealth Office and Buckingham Palace. Such visits are paid for mainly by the Foreign Office, although the host countries may also make a contribution.

FACING PAGE, ABOVE: *Wherever The Queen travels abroad, meeting people, whoever they are, is always important. This little girl in Victoria, British Columbia, was delighted to present Her Majesty with a special posy of flowers . . .*

FACING PAGE, BELOW: *. . . while simply getting close to The Queen is enough for others, such as these young people in Melbourne, Australia.*

ABOVE: *The Queen's travels take her to the most far-flung places to meet all her people, including the citizens of Kathmandu, Nepal, whom she greeted from her ceremonial carriage. It was her second visit to the World's highest nation – her first including a rare ride on an elephant.*

BELOW LEFT: *In 1985 The Queen made an extensive tour of the West Indies, during which she met the Commonwealth Heads of Government at their conference in the Bahamas. Here she is seen arriving at St. Kitts.*

BELOW RIGHT: *In 1983 Mother Teresa of Calcutta received the Order of Merit from Her Majesty The Queen for her work among India's poor. Only four other non-Britons have held this award, the highest in the Sovereign's personal gift.*

## The Queen on Tour

On major tours, whether in the Commonwealth or other foreign countries, The Queen will usually fly to her first destination and then travel between various ports of call in the Royal Yacht *Britannia*. Launched in 1953, *Britannia* is thought to be the seventy-fifth ship provided for the personal use of the Sovereign. She carries a royal barge, in which the royal party may go ashore, two motor boats, a motor cutter, two motor whalers, two motor dinghies, and can accommodate a royal car. She is the only ship in the Royal Navy whose commanding officer is an admiral – the Flag officer Royal Yachts, currently Rear Admiral John Garnier. When the Royal Family are on board, a special quiet routine is observed: all orders are given by signal, not shouted, and soft shoes are worn by the crew of 21 officers and 256 sailors.

One of the greatest advantages of *Britannia* is that receptions can be held on board to return hospitality offered to The Queen by the host country. Up to 200 guests can be accommodated at a cocktail reception, or 40 at a formal dinner. A Royal Marine band is carried on all overseas voyages, and the highlight of many an evening is when the band, in full ceremonial dress, beats retreat on the quayside as The Queen and her guests line the rail of the yacht.

Sometimes during royal tours, British businessmen are able to exploit the goodwill engendered during The Queen's visit by inviting local businessmen to a sea day on board the Royal Yacht during which seminars can be held to promote bilateral trade. The sea day from Shanghai during The Queen's visit to China in 1986 was particularly successful.

*Britannia* is also used for royal honeymoons and most years takes the Royal Family on a cruise round the Western Isles of Scotland before they start their holiday at Balmoral, a voyage believed to be The Queen's favourite relaxation.

On a major tour The Queen will have an entourage of about 45. She will be accompanied by two of her Private Secretaries, her Press Secretary and an Equerry. Also in attendance will be two ladies-in-waiting, one of whom may be the Mistress of the Robes, together with a member of the medical household, clerks and secretaries, maids, footmen and a hairdresser.

A supply of gifts is taken on all tours to show The Queen's appreciation of the work done by the host nation in their organisation. Cuff-links engraved with the Royal Cypher for men, similarly inscribed brooches for ladies, and photographs framed in a variety of materials from leather to heavy silver are often given. Other members of the Royal Family carry stocks of presents inscribed with their own monograms.

While The Queen is on tour abroad, Counsellors of State act on her behalf, for example by giving the Royal Assent to Acts of Parliament, or holding audiences. Two of the six Counsellors of State (the Duke of Edinburgh, Queen Elizabeth the Queen Mother, the Prince of Wales, the Duke of York, Prince Edward and the Princess Royal) are required to act together in each instance.

ABOVE: *Portugal is Britain's oldest ally. When The Queen visited that country she received a special mark of respect from students at the University of Evora. They draped a gown around the Sovereign's shoulders during the University's cloaking ceremony.*

FACING PAGE ABOVE: *Travelling by war canoe from the Royal Yacht* Britannia *towards a Pacific Island might be unusual for a British monarch, but riding in the same boat shoulder high through the streets of the Island of Tuvalu was even more extraordinary.*

RIGHT: *Another more momentous first for a British monarch was The Queen's visit to China and Hong Kong in 1986. In addition to being a visit to one of the world's oldest civilisations, it set the seal on the agreement between Britain and China over the future of the Colony of Hong Kong. The Queen is seen here inspecting a Gurkha Guard of Honour on her arrival in Hong Kong from China.*

RIGHT: *King Hussein of Jordan has a long-standing personal friendship with the British Royal Family. The King and his American-born wife Noor escorted The Queen and Prince Philip on an informal tour of the ancient city of Petra during a recent visit.*

## Royal Ambassador

Besides her visits to Commonwealth countries, The Queen has during her reign made numerous State Visits to other countries abroad. Such visits are usually made at the invitation of foreign heads of state and on the advice of the Foreign Office, for diplomatic reasons. A Foreign Office minister accompanies The Queen to attend to political and trade matters.

The Queen never makes a State Visit more than once to the same foreign head of state. If the head of state changes, she can then make another visit to the country. Moreover, she does not make a private visit to a country before she has visited it officially. The same principle applies to visits to Britain by foreign heads of state.

When a foreign head of state makes a State Visit to Britian, The Queen acts as hostess, organising his entertainment and having him to stay at one of her residences. For example, when King Fahd of Saudia Arabia came to Britain in 1987 he stayed at Buckingham Palace, where a glittering banquet was held in the King's honour. In 1986, King Juan Carlos and Queen Sofia of Spain were entertained at Windsor Castle; despite the formalities, this was almost a family occasion since the British and Spanish royal families are very closely connected, through their common line of descent from Queen Victoria.

Therefore, when one considers the effect of her wide understanding of diplomacy and international affairs, combined with her hospitality and great personal charm, it is easy to believe that The Queen creates more goodwill for Britain in a single visit than an army of Foreign Office officials could achieve in a much longer period.

ABOVE: *Every year The Queen receives State Visits to Britain by one or two foreign Heads of State. The Amir of Bahrain, His Highness Shaikh Isa bin Sulman Al-Khalifa, was greeted by The Queen at the splendidly decorated Royal Pavilion in the Home Park at Windsor before being driven to the Castle in the 1902 State Landau.*

FACING PAGE, BELOW: *The Queen welcomes The President of the United States, Mr Ronald Reagan, and Mrs Nancy Reagan to a banquet at Windsor Castle. Prince Philip is wearing the Windsor uniform, with its distinctive red collar and cuffs, introduced by King George III.*

ABOVE: *The splendour of the State Banquet is a key feature of all State Visits to Britain. At these glittering functions The Queen honours her foreign guests with the very best that royal hospitality can provide. Pictured here is the State Banquet for the President of the United States in St. George's Hall at Windsor Castle.*

LEFT: *However, this hospitality is reciprocated by the visitors. When King Fahd of Saudi Arabia made a State Visit to Britain in 1987, during which he stayed at Buckingham Palace, he thanked The Queen by giving a banquet for her at Claridge's Hotel in London, where he is pictured welcoming The Queen and Prince Philip.*

13

## The Prince Philip, Duke of Edinburgh

As The Queen's consort, Prince Philip, Duke of Edinburgh, does not play any part in the constitutional side of her life; however, he assists her in her role as hostess and accompanies her on overseas tours, seeing himself as a link between Her Majesty and the people.

Prince Philip also plays an outstanding role in the life of the nation in his own right, undertaking over 250 public engagements annually. He is patron or president of several hundred organisations, with a particular interest in the services, young people, sport, and the conservation of the environment in the face of technological development.

Before his marriage to Princess Elizabeth in 1947, His Royal Highness served in the Royal Navy, in which he now holds the rank of Admiral of the Fleet. He is also a Field Marshal in the Army and a Marshal of the Air Force in the RAF, and holds many senior offices in the Commonwealth armed services. In addition, he is colonel-in-chief of 15 regiments at home and throughout the Commonwealth. Prince Philip is an accomplished pilot, qualified to fly many different types of aircraft, including helicopters.

Prince Philip's work with young people focuses on the Duke of Edinburgh's Award Scheme, which aims to 'encourage in the individual the spirit of voluntary service, self-reliance and perseverance, a sense of responsibility and the pursuit of hobbies and other leisure activities'.

Prince Philip's own interest in sport is well known. After giving up polo because of a wrist injury he took up carriage driving, a sport which he was largely responsible for developing in Britain; he represents Britain in international driving events. He is also an accomplished helmsman and admiral of several yacht clubs.

Perhaps technological development and its impact on the natural world is the Duke of Edinburgh's greatest interest. It is this which has led to his long involvement with the World Wildlife Fund. Under his patronage the Fund's first National Appeal was launched by Britain in 1961, and in 1981 he became President of World Wildlife Fund International. He has travelled very widely in this capacity and has written a number of books and articles on this subject. His latest book is *Machines, Men and Sacred Cows* (1984).

Prince Philip has used his strong personality to create an important and individual role for himself out of the perhaps difficult position of consort to The Queen. His energy and enthusiasm for numerous projects have benefited many organisations and he is a source of great support and encouragement for all the members of his family.

TOP: *The Duke of Edinburgh is a skilful carriage driver who has represented England in international events such as the International Driving Championships at Windsor in 1986.*

ABOVE: *Prince Philip also travels extensively as President of the World Wildlife Fund. He is passionately concerned about the impact of technological development on the natural world. This picture was taken during his visit to Chitwan Park, Nepal.*

## Queen Elizabeth The Queen Mother

Born in 1900, the daughter of the 14th Earl of Strathmore, Lady Elizabeth Bowes-Lyon, married the Duke of York, later King George VI, in 1923. Since then, both as Queen Consort and as Queen Mother, her unfailing commitment to the service of the United Kingdom and the Commonwealth, her very real concern and keen interest in everything she undertakes has endeared her to people everywhere. Gracious and charming, she is always ready with a smile and an extra wave of her elegantly gloved hand for the admiring crowds.

Although over 85, she still carries out more than 100 public engagements every year and her stamina saps the strength of those half her age. She is associated as president or patron with about 300 charities and other bodies, among them the British Red Cross Society, Dr Barnardo's Homes, the Girl Guides Association, the Royal Horticultural Society, the National Trust, the RSPCA and the YWCA. She acts as a Counsellor of State when The Queen is absent from the United Kingdom, and has performed many investitures on her behalf.

The Queen Mother is colonel-in-chief of eight regiments in the United Kingdom – 1st The Queen's Dragoon Guards, The Queen's Own Hussars, the 9th/12th Royal Lancers (Prince of Wales's), the King's Regiment, the Royal Anglian Regiment, the Light Infantry, the Black Watch (Royal Highland Regiment) and the Royal Army Medical Corps – as well as a number of Commonwealth regiments.

TOP: *Britain's maritime tradition is marked here by Prince Philip as he inspects the newest generation of the Royal Navy at their passing-out parade at Dartmouth. Prince Philip served in the Royal Navy before his marriage and now holds the rank of Admiral of the Fleet.*

LEFT: *Like many members of the Royal Family, Prince Philip has life-long links with the sea. He is a keen yachtsman and a skilled helmsman. He regularly races during the Cowes Week regatta when the Royal Yacht* Britannia *is a familiar sight anchored in the Solent.*

She is also Commandant-in-Chief of the RAF Central Flying School, the WRNS, WRAC and WRAF, and of the Nursing Corps and Divisions of the St. John Ambulance Brigade. In 1955 she was elected Chancellor of London University, a post now held by her grand-daughter the Princess Royal, and in 1967 she became the first Chancellor of Dundee University. In 1978 she was the first woman to be appointed Lord Warden and Admiral of the Cinque Ports and Constable of Dover Castle.

When in London, the Queen Mother lives at Clarence House, near Buckingham Palace, and her household there is made up of many old friends, some of whom have served her for years. Among these is Ruth, Lady Fermoy, grandmother of the Princess of Wales, who is one of her ladies-in-waiting. The Queen Mother usually spends her weekends at Royal Lodge, Windsor, often with Princess Margaret and her children. New Year is always spent with The Queen and her family at Sandringham and in August she goes to Scotland, staying either at Birkhall on the Balmoral estate or at her own Castle of Mey in Caithness.

The Queen Mother is a keen racing enthusiast, particularly of National Hunt racing, and she has owned a number of steeplechasers. She also enjoys music, gardening and fishing for salmon in the River Dee at Balmoral.

THE CENTREFOLD PICTURES

FACING PAGE 16, TOP: *The Princess of Wales with Prince William and Prince Henry at home in their Drawing Room at Kensington Palace.*

FACING PAGE 16, BOTTOM: *The Prince and Princess of Wales and the Duke and Duchess of York enjoying their skiing holiday at Klosters, Switzerland in February 1987.*

CENTRE OPENING: *The Duchess of York (left) at Denbigh Place, Westminster when she planted a tree for the Westminster Tree and Preservation Trust. The Princess of Wales (right) during her visit to Italy with the Prince of Wales.*

INSIDE: *The Duke and Duchess of York (left) outside Clarence House on the occasion of the 86th birthday of Queen*

*Elizabeth the Queen Mother. A delightful portrait (centre left) of the Prince and Princess of Wales in their Drawing Room at Kensington Palace. The Queen (centre right) enjoying her State Visit to Portugal (Britain's oldest ally). Queen Elizabeth the Queen Mother (right) always manages to look sunny, even on a rainy day.*

ABOVE: *An informal portrait of H.R.H. The Duke of Edinburgh.*

## The Prince of Wales

The Prince of Wales's full style and titles are: *His Royal Highness Prince Charles Philip Arthur George, Knight of the Garter, Knight of the Order of the Thistle, Knight Grand Cross of the Order of the Bath, Privy Counsellor, Prince of Wales and Earl of Chester, Duke of Cornwall and Rothesay, Earl of Carrick and Baron of Renfrew, Lord of the Isles and Great Steward of Scotland.*

He was invested as Prince of Wales by The Queen at Caernarfon Castle in 1969, spending the preceding term at the University College of Wales in Aberystwyth in order to learn the Welsh language. Since his Investiture he has taken his responsibilities towards the Principality very seriously. In 1971 he launched the Prince of Wales' Committee for Wales, which aims to promote projects to improve the Welsh environment and to increase understanding and appreciation of particular areas, and in 1976 he became Chancellor of the University of Wales.

After graduating in 1970 from Trinity College, Cambridge, where he read archaeology, anthropology and history, the Prince followed the Royal Family tradition of a career in the armed services. He was attached to the RAF for a period of five months in 1971 in order to bring his flying to 'wings' standard, and then entered the Royal Navy through the Royal Naval College, Dartmouth. While in the senior service he qualified as helicopter pilot. In 1976 he retired from active service after commanding the minehunter HMS

TOP LEFT: *The Prince of Wales is a keen and skilful polo player. The sport demands excellent horsemanship coupled with a good eye for the ball. Here he is seen in action during a match in Rutland.*

TOP RIGHT: *The Prince makes it his business to be as knowledgeable as possible on a wide range of technological and industrial skills, travelling widely around the United Kingdom to do so. At the dedication of The Phillips Petroleum Group's Maureen production platform at Loch Kishorn, he meets oil rig workers and finds out about the problems of working in the North Sea oil and gas fields.*

ABOVE: *The Prince of Wales meets rock star Rod Stewart at a Gala Concert in aid of The Prince's Trust.*

17

*Bronington*, and in 1977 was promoted to the rank of commander, and also to wing-commander in the RAF. The following year he added a qualification as a parachutist to his already impressive record. He is Colonel of the Welsh Guards, and Colonel-in-Chief of the Royal Regiment of Wales (24th/41st Foot), the Cheshire Regiment, the Parachute Regiment, the 2nd King Edward VII Own Goorkhas, the Gordon Highlanders and a number of Commonwealth regiments.

In civilian life the Prince carries out some 300 public engagements a year, in addition to frequent trips abroad. Like all members of the Royal Family he is involved with a number of charitable organisations, and has a particular interest in working with the young. He is President of the Royal Jubilee Trusts, which incorporates the Queen's Silver Jubilee Trust set up in 1977 with the aim of encouraging young people to give service to other members of the community, and of the Prince's Trust, which 'helps young people to help themselves', for instance to set up their own businesses. In 1982 he started the Youth Business Initiative which now, together with the Youth Enterprise Scheme, is part of The Prince's Youth Business Trust. The Prince is also President of the United World Colleges, a network of sixth-form colleges established throughout the world by Kurt Hahn, the founder of his old school, Gordonstoun.

Like his father, the Prince is keenly interested in wildlife and conservation. One particular cause which has benefited from his special concern is that of the endangered heath fritillary butterfly. Working with the Cornwall Trust for Nature Conservation and the Nature Conservancy Council, the Prince had a plantation of conifers removed from his land in the Duchy of Cornwall in order to restore the butterfly's natural habitat and enable it to breed. He takes an interest in agriculture on his estate in Cornwall and enjoys working there.

Another of the Prince's abiding interests is history and archaeology. He is President of the Mary Rose Trust, and in the months leading up to the raising in 1982 of the *Mary Rose*, Henry VIII's flagship which sank in the Solent in 1545, the Prince dived several times to see the wreck and the lifting preparations for himself.

Prince Charles is an active and enthusiastic sportsman and seems prepared to try his hand at almost any outdoor sport – from windsurfing and skiing to his well-known interest in polo-playing.

Although the Prince of Wales will accede to the throne one day, that day may well be far off. In the meantime he has had to come to terms with the rather indeterminate role of the Heir Apparent. However, it is clear that he is following the family example of wide-ranging interests and involvement, in preparation for a destiny which he evidently intends to face with the same dedication and devotion with which his mother has faced hers, ever since the afternoon in 1952 at Treetops in Kenya when she was told that she had become Queen.

ABOVE: *The Prince of Wales is an accomplished artist who has had one of his works exhibited at the Summer Exhibition at The Royal Academy. He takes his sketch pad on his travels and did not miss the opportunity to draw the famous temples and gardens of Kyoto in Japan.*

FACING PAGE, ABOVE LEFT: *The Princess of Wales arriving for a service at Westminster Abbey.*

## The Princess of Wales

From the moment she said 'I will' at St. Paul's Cathedral on 29 July 1981, the Princess of Wales became a member of the 'Family Firm' and henceforth was expected to carry out her share of public duties.

Understandably shy at first, Her Royal Highness has had to learn to deal with the problems of constantly being in the focus of the public spotlight. Within a year of her marriage she became one of the most popular and certainly the most photographed woman in the world.

The Princess of Wales's naturalness, her charm, her evident concern for the sick and disabled, and her fondness for children have won her admirers everywhere. She does not seem to mind how many people want to touch her and talk to her; she is not deterred by grubby childish fingers touching her clothes, and when talking to children or people in wheelchairs she will sit on her heels so that she can talk to them on the same level.

Through her special love for children she has become involved with a number of children's organisations such as Dr Barnado's, the Pre-School Playgroups Association, and the National Children's Orchestra. She is particularly concerned for the sick and disabled and her public engagements include frequent visits to hospitals as well as schools and youth centres.

The Princess of Wales also helps to promote her husband's charities and shares his special relationship with Wales. On their first tour of the Principality together, soon after their wedding, Her Royal Highness delighted everyone by showing she had learnt some Welsh when she received the Freedom of the City of Cardiff. She is Patron of the highly successful Welsh National Opera and the Swansea Festival of Music and the Arts, and President of the Welsh Craft Council.

Heads are turned and the fashion writers take note every time the Princess of Wales appears. Even before her wedding, the 'Lady Diana' hairstyle was to be seen all over the world. Low-heeled shoes then became a necessity for every fashionable girl as the tall Princess set a new trend. The best young British designers have found her the best possible boost to their success. Hats, too, have been made popular again by Her Royal Highness, and milliners all over the country are grateful to her influence as ladies rush to buy copies.

The Princess is a loving wife and a devoted mother to the two young Princes William and Henry, born in 1982 and 1984 respectively. She has a busy schedule of public engagements of her own, in addition to her many visits at home and abroad together with the Prince of Wales, but spends as much time as possible at home with her children at Kensington Palace, or at Highgrove, their country home in Gloucestershire.

Since her marriage the Princess has matured beyond her years and captured the nation's heart. She has learned to withstand the unceasing pressures of her position and is now more clearly seen as the future Queen Consort, a prospect hopefully distant.

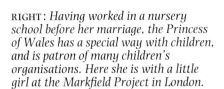

RIGHT: *Having worked in a nursery school before her marriage, the Princess of Wales has a special way with children, and is patron of many children's organisations. Here she is with a little girl at the Markfield Project in London.*

LEFT: *The Princess with The Amir of Bahrain during her visit to the Gulf States in 1986 with the Prince of Wales.*

FACING PAGE, ABOVE: *Over 10,000 excited children greeted the Royal couple when they arrived at the spectacular Sydney Opera House during a visit to Australia.*

FACING PAGE, BELOW LEFT: *The Princess's nautical outfit complements the Prince of Wales in his uniform as Commander in the Royal Navy during their visit to a naval dockyard at La Spezia, Italy.*

ABOVE: *The Prince (whose titles include Lord of the Isles and Great Steward of Scotland) and Princess are seen in North Uist during a visit to the Outer Hebrides.*

ABOVE: *The Prince and Princess of Wales like to spend as much time as possible with their children, either at Kensington Palace or at their country home at Highgrove in Gloucestershire. Princes William and Henry play with their father in Kensington Palace.*

RIGHT: *Their mother is in reflective mood at a desert picnic during her visit with the Prince to Saudi Arabia.*

RIGHT: *The Princess was on hand to see Prince William off to his first day at Wetherby School in London.*

FAR RIGHT: *Prince William and Prince Henry, second and third respectively in line to the throne, enjoy dressing up in the replica parachute combat gear which was a gift from the Parachute Regiment.*

## The Duke and Duchess of York

Just before Prince Andrew married Sarah Ferguson in Westminster Abbey on 23 July 1986 it was announced that The Queen had been pleased to bestow the ancient royal dukedom of York on her son. The immediate previous holder of this dukedom, traditionally granted to the second son of the Sovereign, was the Prince's grandfather, King George VI.

Like his father, the Duke of Edinburgh, and his two brothers, Prince Andrew was educated at Gordonstoun. Long before he left school he had decided that his career would be in the Royal Navy. Before taking his A levels he spent six months at Lakefield College, Ontario. In 1978 he joined Prince Charles on a parachute jumping course at RAF Brize Norton in Oxfordshire and both were awarded their parachute badges. A year later the Prince joined the Royal Naval College at Dartmouth.

Since the early days of aviation the Royal Family have been very 'air-minded'. In 1919, as Prince Albert, King George VI became its first member to become an RAF pilot. The Duke of Windsor was a qualified pilot as are Prince Philip and his three sons. Continuing the family tradition and determined to understand better her husband's work, the Duchess of York took flying lessons shortly after her marriage and now holds a private pilot's licence.

Prince Andrew received his wings as a helicopter pilot at RNAS Culdrose in 1981. Within 12 months he was plunged into active warfare in the Falklands campaign flying from the aircraft carrier HMS *Invincible* on hazardous anti-submarine and missile decoy operations. His service in the Falklands attracted much attention – as did his social life, and he was widely regarded as the world's most eligible bachelor.

Andrew and Sarah first met as children and had known each other for some years, but it was not until 1985 that their friendship blossomed into courtship. In June that year Miss Ferguson was amongst the guests invited by The Queen to Windsor Castle during Royal Ascot week. This was on the suggestion of the Princess of Wales; she and Sarah had long been friends and the Princess did much to foster the romance, of which the public had its first hint when the Prince was seen in the Royal Box with a strikingly beautiful red-head.

In the following January Sarah was again a guest of the Royal Family for

TOP: *Since their wedding in 1986 the spontaneity and sense of fun shown by the Duke and Duchess of York have made them extremely popular. While both follow their own careers, they also undertake their full share of royal duties.*

ABOVE: *One of their 1987 visits was to Jersey in the Channel Islands to open the 33rd Jersey International Air Rally – a very appropriate task for this very 'air-minded' couple. Her personal style has enabled the Duchess to take easily to the art and practice of the royal 'walkabout'.*

the New Year holiday at Sandringham, and, after a visit to HMS *Brazen*, the ship in which Prince Andrew was then serving, and a skiing holiday at Klosters in Switzerland with the Prince and Princess of Wales, the full beam of the media searchlight was focused on her. The world and his wife had decided that Prince Andrew should marry this spirited and charming young woman and nobody was surprised when, in March 1986, Buckingham Palace made the formal announcement.

The wedding in Westminster Abbey was a spectacular royal event and during the service the bride promised to obey her husband. The honeymoon was spent in the Azores and appropriately the groom piloted the new BAe 146 aircraft which had just been delivered to The Queen's Flight.

Since their marriage the Duchess of York has taken on an increasing list of royal engagements and the Duke has resumed his full-time naval duties as an instructor in helicopter warfare. Like many married naval officers he and his wife live outside service accommodation and they have rented Chideock Manor in Dorset.

ABOVE LEFT and TOP: *The Duke and Duchess of York's busy lifestyles sometimes mean the Duke's work as a Royal Naval Lieutenant and Royal duties give them little time together. But family life is important to them, and they are popular members of the Royal Family.*

24

ABOVE: *This picture taken shortly before their wedding shows the couple together at the Royal Aero Club Digital Schneider Trophy Air Race on the Isle of Wight. In addition to being a professional pilot in the Royal Navy, Prince Andrew is also President of the Club.*

TOP LEFT: *The Duchess of York arrives at Claridge's Hotel with her husband for a banquet given by King Fahd of Saudi Arabia.*

ABOVE: *The couple in Weymouth not long before their marriage.*

LEFT: *Like her husband, the Duchess has now qualified as a pilot. Here, with her instructor Colin Beckwith, she holds her private pilot's licence.*

ABOVE: *The Princess Royal attending a banquet given by the King of Saudi Arabia.*

LEFT: *The Queen's youngest son, the Prince Edward, with his father beside him, presents the prizes at a charity event.*

FACING PAGE, ABOVE: *The Princess Royal has been a highly active President of the Save the Children Fund, working both to promote it and help its work all over the world. A recent journey through Africa took the Princess to see for herself the Fund's work bringing succour to children in drought-stricken areas.*

FACING PAGE, BELOW LEFT: *The Princess is also Chancellor of London University and is seen here attending a degree ceremony at the Royal Albert Hall.*

FACING PAGE, BELOW RIGHT: *As Chief Commandant of WRNS the Princess Royal visits HMS Royal Arthur.*

## The Prince Edward

Prince Edward's early years followed much the same pattern as those of his brothers. At Gordonstoun he achieved the distinction of becoming head boy and the reputation of being a scholar. Before going up to Jesus College Cambridge in 1983 to study modern history, he spent two years as a house tutor at Wanganui Collegiate School in New Zealand. He learned to fly at RAF Cranwell and obtained his private pilot's licence while still at school.

The Prince had joined the Royal Marines in 1983 and in September 1986, having come down from Cambridge with a degree in history, he began what is probably the toughest training course in the British armed forces, that for Commando Officers. However, seven months later, after much anxious deliberation in the full glare of the public spotlight, and in the face of the disappointment of his family and the Corps, he decided to resign his commission. It was clearly a difficult and courageous decision to break a long-standing family tradition and also admit a mistake over his choice of career.

Prince Edward has a particular interest in projects for helping young people and for some years he has been an enthusiastic worker for the Duke of Edinburgh's Award Scheme. He is himself a Gold Award winner and in 1986 he chaired the Award's 30th Anniversary celebrations which were highlighted by an 800 mile walk from Buckingham Palace to Balmoral in which 2,000 walkers took part. Two special BBC 1 programmes on the Award Scheme were written and presented by Prince Edward in 1987. They received wide acclaim and did much to promote public awareness of the scheme. The programmes also demonstrated the Prince's ability as a communicator; taken with his enthusiasm for drama and the theatre, they perhaps point the way to his future.

## The Princess Royal

Like the other members of the Royal Family, the Princess Royal combines a wide variety of roles in her public and private lives. Like them also, she has strong connections with the armed services and is colonel-in-chief of several regiments, both in Britain and in the Commonwealth, including the 14th/20th King's Hussars, the Royal Corps of Signals, the Worcestershire and Sherwood Foresters and the 8th Canadian Hussars. She pays regular visits to her regiments and particularly enjoys being with them when they are on manoeuvres, as it gives her the opportunity to try out some of their equipment: indeed she has even driven a 50-ton tank over an assault course in Germany.

The Princess is also Chief Commandant of the WRNS, and numbers the WRNS Benevolent Fund among the various organisations of which she is president. Others include the British Academy of Film and Television Arts and the Save the Children Fund. For this latter organisation she has worked tirelessly, travelling extensively to visit refugee camps and the famine and war-ridden areas of the world, especially in Africa and the Middle East. It was largely in recognition of this work that The Queen bestowed upon her, in June 1987, the title reserved for the Sovereign's eldest daughter – the Princess Royal.

Another favourite charity is the Riding for the Disabled Association. The

Princess Royal is, of course, a well-known horsewoman, winning the European Three-Day Event Championship in 1971 and riding for Britain in the Olympic Games in Montreal in 1976. Although she has taken part in fewer competitive events since the birth of her children, Peter in 1977 and Zara in 1981, she is still a keen rider and her day usually begins with a work-out with her horses.

The Princess's husband, Captain Mark Phillips, is also a well-known competitive rider, and takes part in top-class three-day events on behalf of the Range Rover Team which he manages. Although he sometimes accompanies Her Royal Highness on overseas tours, he spends most of his time working the farm on the Gatcombe estate in Gloucestershire which was given to the couple by The Queen.

## The Princess Margaret, Countess of Snowdon

The Princess Margaret, Countess of Snowdon, The Queen's sister, is devoted to the arts and any function which aims to help the opera or ballet is almost certain to find a champion in her. She has been President of the Royal Ballet since 1956 and is also President of the Sadlers Wells Foundation and Patron of the London Festival Ballet. The Princess thoroughly enjoys all types of theatrical event and has a wide circle of friends in the profession. She is a talented mimic herself and at private parties requires little persuasion to perform one of her impersonations.

On the more serious side, the many organisations with which the Princess is involved include several concerned with children's welfare, among them Dr Barnardo's, the Sunshine Homes and Schools for Blind Children and the NSPCC. She is Chancellor of Keele University, and colonel-in-chief or deputy colonel-in-chief of seven regiments.

Since her divorce from Lord Snowdon, Princess Margaret has spent more time than ever with Queen Elizabeth the Queen Mother, often joining her at Royal Lodge, Windsor, for the weekend. During the week she lives at Kensington Palace with her daughter, Lady Sarah. Lord Snowdon continues to see his children regularly and remains on friendly terms with the Royal Family.

Princess Margaret's children have both decided to make careers for themselves outside the royal circle. David,

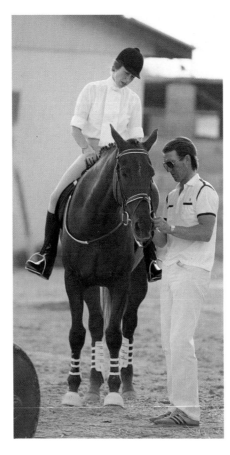

LEFT: *The Princess Royal used her international equestrian skills to compete at the Dubai Horse show, with the help of her husband Captain Mark Phillips, as a fund raising venture for the Save the Children Fund.*

BELOW: *All the Princess Royal's family are interested in horses, as this picture of the Princess and her two children Peter and Zara at the Windsor Horse Trials shows.*

Viscount Linley, studied carpentry at the John Makepeace School for Craftsmen in Dorset and has since formed a successful business partnership with three of his fellow-students, making and selling furniture.

Lady Sarah Armstrong-Jones has blossomed into one of the most vivacious of the younger generation of royal cousins, and, having inherited her parents' artistic inclination, has studied art and design at the Middlesex Polytechnic and the Royal Academy.

FACING PAGE ABOVE: *A sparkling portrait of Princess Margaret by her former husband, the photographer Lord Snowdon.*

FACING PAGE, BELOW: *Princess Margaret with her son and daughter, Viscount Linley and Lady Sarah Armstrong-Jones.*

## Princess Alice, Duchess of Gloucester

Three generations of the Gloucester family live in apartments at Kensington Palace. Princess Alice, Duchess of Gloucester, daughter of the Duke of Buccleuch and Queensberry, married Prince Henry, Duke of Gloucester, in 1935. Like the Queen Mother, she is into her eighties, but she continues to attend frequent public engagements on behalf of the 74 organisations of which she is patron or president. She has close connections with the armed services, and much of her work is in aid of servicemen's welfare organisations. Princess Alice is a talented watercolourist and has held several exhibitions of her work.

ABOVE: *Princess Alice, Duchess of Gloucester, talking to Chelsea Pensioner Sergeant J. McClellan at the Park Lane Fair.*

29

## The Duke and Duchess of Gloucester

Princess Alice's son, Richard, Duke of Gloucester, studied at Cambridge and then set up an architect's practice in North London. In 1972 he married a Danish commoner, Birgitte van Deurs, whom he had known at university. Owing to the tragic death of his older brother William in an air crash in 1972, Richard succeeded on the death of his father in 1974 to the title and the responsibility of running the family estate at Barnwell in Northamptonshire. He gave up his work as an architect in order to fulfil his share of royal duties but maintains a close involvement in architecture and history (his other special interest) through his posts as Deputy Chairman of English Heritage (and Chairman of its Grants Advisory Committee) and Trustee of the British Museum.

The Duchess of Gloucester has adapted to the life of a member of the Royal Family in a way which few could have forecast. She heads over 30 organisations and likes to meet the workers of them all as informally as possible. However, she tries to keep as much time as possible free to spend with her children, Alexander, Earl of Ulster, born in 1974, Lady Davina Windsor, who was born in 1977, and Lady Rose Windsor, born in 1980.

ABOVE RIGHT: *The Duchess of Gloucester with two of her children, Lady Davina Windsor and Lady Rose Windsor.*

BELOW: *The Duke and Duchess of Gloucester at a royal banquet in London.*

## The Duke and Duchess of Kent

The Duke of Kent, elder son of the late Prince George, Duke of Kent, and Princess Marina, was educated at Eton and Sandhurst and went on to become a Lieutenant-Colonel in the Royal Scots Dragoon Guards, with whom he served until 1976. He was promoted to the rank of Major-General in 1983. Besides his royal duties – he is patron or president of many organisations, including the RAF Benevolent Fund, the All England Lawn Tennis and Croquet Club, the Leukemia Research Fund and the Royal National Lifeboat Institution – the Duke is Vice-Chairman of the British Overseas Trade Board. An excellent linguist, he travels far and wide on behalf of the British export drive. He is also Chancellor of the University of Surrey. The Duke has been a freemason since 1964 and is now Grand Master of the United Grand Lodge of England. He is president of several masonic charities.

With his wife, formerly Katherine Worsley, he shares a love of music and opera. The Duke is President of the Royal Choral Society and the Duchess is President of the Royal Northern College of Music and also sings with the Bach Choir. The Duchess has the most understanding of attitudes to the elderly, the infirm and the sick, and much of her work is in aid of Age Concern, the Spastics Society and the National Society for Cancer Relief. She is also Patron of the Samaritans, and has even trained as a counsellor for them. In 1965 she became Chancellor of Leeds University.

The eldest of the three children of the Duke and Duchess of Kent, the Earl of St. Andrews, born in 1962, was the first member of the Royal Family to win a scholarship to Eton, and has inherited his father's gift for languages. He is now a post graduate student of history at Cambridge University, and is engaged to fellow student Miss Sylvana Tomaselli, from Canada. Their other two children are Lady Helen Windsor, born in 1964, and Lord Nicholas Windsor, born in 1970.

# Prince and Princess Michael of Kent

Prince Michael is the younger son of the late Duke of Kent and Princess Marina. Like his brother, the Duke of Kent, he was educated at Eton and the Royal Military Academy, Sandhurst, and served in the Royal Hussars and in the Ministry of Defence as a general staff officer in military intelligence. Since leaving the Army he has worked in the City, and is Deputy Chairman of Walbrook Insurance Ltd and of London United Investments, and a Director of Standard Telephones and Cables plc. The Prince and Princess carry out between them well over 100 official engagements a year, to which the Princess always brings a touch of elegance and charm.

Like his brother, Prince Michael is a freemason and in 1985 he was installed as Master of Grand Stewards Lodge. He is fascinated by speed and things mechanical and won the British bobsleigh championship in 1972. He also enjoys motor racing and rally driving: in 1970 he competed in the World Cup Rally from London to Mexico. With this background it is fitting that he should be President of the RAC, the Institute of the Motor Industry and the Motor Industry Research Association. He is also President of SSAFA, the Royal Patriotic Fund Corporation and the Kennel Club, as well as Commonwealth President of the Royal Life Saving Society.

TOP LEFT: *The Duchess of Kent with her daughter Lady Helen Windsor at Covent Garden during The Queen's 60th Birthday Celebrations in 1986.*

TOP RIGHT: *The Duke of Kent in the uniform of the Scots Guards at Sandhurst.*

ABOVE: *Prince and Princess Michael of Kent at the Dorchester Hotel in London.*

ABOVE: *Lord Frederick and Lady Gabriella Windsor, the children of Prince and Princess Michael of Kent, with their family pets.*

31

Princess Michael, formerly Baroness Marie Christine von Reibnitz, married Prince Michael in Vienna in 1978, and the couple have two children, Lord Frederick Windsor, born in 1979, and Lady Gabriella Windsor, born in 1981.

## Princess Alexandra, the Hon. Mrs Angus Ogilvy

An exceedingly popular member of the Royal Family is Princess Alexandra, the Hon. Mrs Angus Ogilvy, daughter of the late Duke of Kent and Princess Marina. As a young woman she did a short nursing course at the Great Ormond Street Hospital for Sick Children, and many of the organisations of which she is patron or president are connected with the nursing profession. These include the British Red Cross Society, Princess Mary's RAF Nursing Service, and the Queen Alexandra's Royal Naval Nursing Service. Her other charities include the Royal Commonwealth Society for the Blind, the Royal Star and Garter Home for Disabled Sailors, Soldiers and Airmen, and the Guide Dogs for the Blind Association. She also has the usual Royal Family services connections and has been an active Chancellor of Lancaster University since its inception in 1964.

In 1963 the Princess married the Hon. Angus Ogilvy, son of the 12th Earl of Airlie, a businessman and director of many companies. His early career was as a captain in the Scots Guards, and he is a member of the Royal Company of Archers, The Queen's Bodyguard for Scotland. He is involved with a number of charities of his own including the Imperial Cancer Research Fund, the National Association of Youth Clubs, and the Scottish Wildlife Trust.

The elder of the Ogilvy children, James, born in 1964, was educated at Eton like his father. Before going up to the University of St Andrews in October 1983 he took up a short-service commission with his father's old regiment. His sister Marina, born in 1966, is a keen pianist and seems destined for a career in the arts.

TOP: *Princess Alexandra brought a touch of royal glamour to RAF Benson when she met the Captain of The Queen's Flight and other officers.*

LEFT: *Princess Alexandra and her husband, the Hon. Angus Ogilvy, at The Guildhall in London.*